The Secret of Transitions

OrangeBooks Publication

1st Floor, Rajhans Arcade, Mall Road, Kohka, Bhilai, Chhattisgarh 490020
Website: **www.orangebooks.in**

First Edition, 2026

ISBN: 978-93-7426-240-5

Price: Rs. 250.00

Printed in India

THE SECRET OF TRANSITIONS

"THE PRICE OF CHANGE"

RATHEESH DIVAKARAN

OrangeBooks Publication
www.orangebooks.in

Introduction
The Price of Change

Once, my sister said to me,

"You have changed a lot."

She has known me since childhood. She can sense even the smallest shift in me. For a long time, I wondered—what was that change she noticed?

At 21, I started my own office as a civil engineering professional. I had no business background, no inherited legacy, and no extraordinary advantage. Yet I performed better than many engineers of my age. Opportunities came looking for me.

Then I stepped into construction. Projects increased. Money flowed. But…

By 32, I had accumulated forty lakh rupees in debt. I got married at 28. To repay debts, we sold my wife's gold. Still, the debt grew out of my control.

But I need to change for living, I am not ready for suicide. Here just I am pausing my story.

Psychologically, real change happens at three levels:

1. **Behaviour level** – What you do
2. **Belief level** – What you think
3. **Identity level** – Who you believe you are

Most people try to change at the behaviour level:

- New habits
- New routines
- New goals

But if identity remains the same, old patterns return.

When I was in debt, my real problem was not money.

It was identity confusion.

I was acting like a successful professional externally, but internally I lacked financial discipline, emotional control, and self-awareness.

At 35, the change that occurred was not financial—it was psychological.

I stopped asking:

“How do I earn more?”

I started asking:

“Who must I become to handle success?”

That question changes everything.

Then, at 35, something changed inside me.

Within one year, I cleared all debts. I built assets. More importantly, I rebuilt myself. The methods I followed, the mindset I adopted, and the inner changes I made transformed my life.

For the past 12 years, I have continued that transformation.

This book is not about overnight success.

It is about evolution.

I am sure.

No greeting, no motivational speech, no magic formula can change your life. Real change requires pain. Not suffering—but discipline.

A bodybuilder does not grow by lifting the heaviest weight on the first day. Growth comes from small, consistent practice.

If you are ready for transformation, this book is for you.

Contents

“You Are More Than a Title—

Discover Who You Truly Are.”

Chapter 1

Self-Realisation-You Are More Than a Title

Before direction, before discipline, before success—there is one question:

Who are you?

Not your name.

Not your job.

Not your reputation.

Who are you beyond your title?

For a long time, I didn't understand this. Until I discovered my true potential, I was below zero—not empty, but negative. Money could not lift me because I didn't know who I was.

Real growth begins with self-awareness.

Everyone is unique.

But being special requires intention.

If you believe you are special, you carry responsibility—to grow into your potential.

Without self-realisation:

- Habits control you.
- Fears guide you.
- Life feels like it is happening to you.

Reflect on These Questions:

1. List 10 personal qualities.
2. Identify 3 core skills.
3. If you lost everything tomorrow, what would you do?
4. If you became very wealthy overnight, what would you do?
5. Where do you want to be in 5 and 10 years? Why?

Clarity may not come instantly. Sit with the questions.

The Path to Transformation

Once you know your 10-year vision, ask:

"What must I change within myself to reach that future?"

The answers may be uncomfortable. That's where growth begins.

Humans are special because we can consciously reshape ourselves.

Transformation begins with self-realisation.

Self-Realisation – Action Plan

1. **Identity Audit (Day 1–3)**
   - Write 10 personal qualities.
   - Circle 5 that truly represent you.
   - Cross out 3 that are actually social labels (job, status, income).

2. **Strength Mapping**
   - List 3 skills that can earn money.
   - List 3 emotional strengths (patience, courage, resilience, etc.).

- Ask one trusted person:

"What is my strongest quality?"

3. Future Self Exercise

- Write a one-page letter from your 10-year future self.
- Describe:
  - Income
  - Health
  - Personality
  - Discipline level
  - Social circle

4. Identity Shift Question (Daily)

Every night ask:

"Did my actions today match the person I want to become?"

“Success isn’t found in a 25th hour; it’s hidden in the 8 hours you currently waste.”

Chapter 2
Reclaim Your Time, Rewrite Your Life

Time is the ultimate equalizer. Whether you are a billionaire or a dreamer, we all receive the same 24 hours. The difference between those who struggle and those who succeed isn't the amount of time they are given—it is the **courage** they use to claim it.

The Shift from Survival to Success

In my earlier days, I lived in the shadow of debt. I spent 95% of my mental energy asking the wrong questions:

- *How will I survive today?*
- *How can I manage these losses?*

When you focus on the hole you're in, you only dig deeper. I had to stop managing my misery and start engineering my exit. I shifted my focus from **surviving debt** to **creating income.** But a mindset shift needs a system to sustain it. That is when I found the **8×8×8 Rule.**

The Rule of Three: Your 24-Hour Revolution

To change your life, you must divide your day into three non-negotiable pillars.

Pillar	Purpose	The Focus
8 Hours	Recovery	Deep, restorative sleep to fuel your brain.
8 Hours	Production	Focused, high-quality work and career growth.
8 Hours	The Soul	Self-improvement, family, and future-building.

The "Third Eight": Where Champions Are Made

Most people throw away their final eight hours. They let it leak into distractions, mindless scrolling, or toxic habits. But this is the "Golden 8." This is where you invest in:

- **Skill Acquisition:** Learning what the market pays for.
- **Vitality:** Prioritizing the fitness that fuels your energy.
- **Connection:** Investing in the people who ground you.
- **Planning:** Designing tomorrow before it arrives.

The Price of Greatness

To follow this rule, you will have to say **"No."**

You will have to disappoint people who want to waste your time. You will have to walk away from habits that no longer serve your vision.

Remember: Your time eventually converts into your currency. It becomes your health. It becomes your legacy. Do not compromise on the only asset you can never buy back.

"Don't just spend your time. Invest it."

“With Direction,

Even Small Steps Take You Far.”

Chapter 3

Direction – The Foundation of Progress

Without direction, effort feels heavy.

Every goal requires clarity in three things:

1. Direction
2. Distance
3. Time

Most people worry about distance and time.

But the real problem is lack of direction.

When direction is unclear, the mind becomes confused.

This confusion creates mental traps.

Common Mental Traps

1. Information Mania

Constantly collecting knowledge without deciding what to follow.

Solution:

Choose one conclusion. Write it down. Repeat:

"This is my reality."

Then move forward.

2. The Knowing–Doing Trap

You know what to do—but don't act.

Solution:

Take small, immediate actions. Tiny steps calm the mind.

3. Achievement Addiction

Always chasing the next goal without celebrating success.

Solution:

Pause. Celebrate. Teach your brain that you are winning.

4. Endless Multitasking

Constant switching drains focus and energy.

Solution:

Add short breaks. Reset between tasks.

5. Excessive Screen Time

Comfort mode weakens effort and creates procrastination.

Solution:

Reduce unnecessary screen use. Protect your focus.

6. Peer Pressure

Blindly following trends and opinions.

Solution:

Set boundaries. Choose friends wisely. Build self-confidence.

With direction, even small steps take you far.

Without direction, effort is wasted.

Direction – Action Plan

1. Define One Primary Goal (Not 5)

Write clearly:

- Direction (What exactly?)
- Distance (How big?)
- Time (By when?)

Example:

"Become debt-free in 18 months."

2. Eliminate Mental Traps (7-Day Reset)

Day 1–2: Delete unnecessary apps.

Day 3–4: Limit screen time to 1 hour for entertainment.

Day 5: Stop multitasking. Work in 45-minute focus blocks.

Day 6: Avoid negative conversations.

Day 7: Review progress and adjust.

3. Weekly Direction Check

Every Sunday:

- What did I move forward?
- What distracted me?
- What must I eliminate next week?

“Pure Intention Is the Foundation of Lasting Success.”

Chapter 4
Intention Must Be Pure

When you decide to change your life, you already understand one thing:

You need direction.

But there is something even more powerful than direction.

Intention.

Direction tells you *where* you are going.

Intention determines *who you become* on the way.

Why Purity of Intention Matters

You may chase money.

You may chase fame.

You may chase recognition.

But if your inner voice says,

"I must make money somehow."

"I must become famous at any cost."

Be careful.

The words *somehow* and *at any cost* are dangerous.

They quietly plant seeds of compromise, shortcuts, and self-destruction.

Success built on impure intention does not last.

It traps you instead of freeing you.

A Lesson in Hidden Motives

A man once shared his "brilliant" business idea with me.

He wanted to open an old-age home.

On the surface, it sounded noble.

Caring for the elderly.

Providing comfort.

Offering dignity in their final years.

His plans were detailed. Structured. Impressive.

But then his tone changed.

He said,

“Wealthy people don’t have time to care for their parents. They’ll bring them to us and pay whatever we charge. And if we handle things cleverly, some residents might even transfer their property to us. After all… they won’t live much longer.”

In that moment, everything became clear.

He was not seeing an opportunity through the eyes of service.

He was seeing it through the eyes of greed.

And greed always reveals itself.

He started his venture but now its in the safe custody of Bank that which he borrowed money.

When you look at opportunity like a vulture—circling, calculating, waiting to benefit from weakness—you may gain money, but you lose something far more valuable:

Integrity.

The Law of Clean Growth

Yes, you must grow.

Yes, you must move forward.

Yes, you must succeed.

There is no doubt about that.

But growth without purity is fragile.

It collapses under its own weight.

Pure intention means:

- You create value, not exploitation.
- You serve, not manipulate.
- You build, not extract.

When your intention is clean:

- Your confidence becomes stronger.
- Your decisions become clearer.
- Your success becomes sustainable.

And most importantly—you can look at yourself with respect.

Ask Yourself

Before starting any goal, pause and ask:

- Why am I really doing this?
- If nobody praised me, would I still do it?
- If profit were delayed, would I still believe in it?
- Does this idea uplift others—or only benefit me?

Your answers will reveal your true intention.

Remember This

Money earned with purity brings peace.

Money earned through greed brings fear.

Fame built on service builds legacy.

Fame built on manipulation builds anxiety.

You are not just building success.

You are building your character.

And character determines how long success stays.

Final Truth

Direction gives you movement.

Discipline gives you strength.

But **pure intention gives you lasting success.**

Guard it. Protect it. Build with it

"Discipline Is the Price You Pay for the Future You Want."

Chapter 5

Discipline – The Bridge to Success

Success is not accidental.

It is the by-product of intentional effort.

Discipline is the restriction we place on our choices.

We know what is right and wrong.

But we often choose pleasure over growth. Even that is wrong.

The world offers countless distractions. Businesses people making profit from our lack of control. Whenever you scroll your mobile phone some people will get money.

Discipline is not punishment.

It is choosing long-term happiness over short-term pleasure.

Examples:

- Waking up early — breaks your comfort.
- Reducing screen time — reduces your easy pleasure.
- Daily exercise — challenges the body and grab your pleasurable time.

Hooo then where you to stick on?.

But each intentional action strengthens self-control.

Discipline is the temporary loss of pleasure for lifelong gain.

Discipline – Action Plan

1. 30-Day Discipline Challenge

Choose only 3 habits:

- Wake-up time
- Exercise (minimum 20 mins)
- 1 hour focused work

Do not add more.

2. Pleasure Awareness Exercise

For one week:

- Track where your time goes.
- Highlight "pleasure activities."
- Reduce them by 20%.

3. Delayed Gratification Rule

Before any impulse action, ask:

"Will this help my 5-year future?"

Pause for 60 seconds before deciding

“Choose Lasting Happiness Over Temporary Pleasure.”

Chapter 6

Happiness – Temporary vs. Permanent

Happiness looks different for everyone.

But there are two types:

Temporary Happiness

Driven by impulses and chemical highs (dopamine, serotonin, oxytocin, endorphins).

This often leads to addiction.

The body doesn't distinguish between healthy reward and harmful habit. It just wants repetition.

Permanent Happiness

Steady. Deep. Unshakable.

To reach it, we must sacrifice temporary pleasure.

Addictions and distractions block the path to lasting fulfilment.

Do not trade lifelong success for momentary comfort.

Happiness – Action Plan

1. Dopamine Control Plan

Avoid for 14 days:

- Excess social media
- Unnecessary scrolling
- Junk entertainment

Replace with:

- Reading
- Walking
- Skill building

2. Permanent Happiness Builder

Daily:

- 20 mins exercise
- 20 mins learning

- 10 mins silence/reflection

3. Addiction Awareness

Write:

- 3 habits that give temporary pleasure.
- 1 long-term goal each habit is blocking

"Do not fight your mind—
align it with your vision."

Chapter 7

Satisfy the Mind – Don't Punish It

Discipline without convincing the mind will not last.

You cannot force yourself into permanent change.

You must fall in love with your goal.

Small mental exercises matter.

Consistency matters more than intensity.

A resilient mind is built through steady, simple practices.

Strength does not mean harshness.

It means alignment.

Satisfy the Mind – Action Plan

1. Fall in Love with Your Goal

Create:

- Vision board (digital or printed)
- Phone wallpaper of your goal
- Write your goal daily for 30 days

2. Micro-Win Strategy

Break big goal into:

- Monthly target
- Weekly target
- Daily action

Celebrate small wins.

3. Mental Resilience Practice

When failure happens:

Write:

- What happened?
- What did I learn?

- What will I improve?

No self-criticism allowed

"You don't find role models—

you become one."

Chapter 8
Become Your Own Role Model

Yes, it is possible.

And it is necessary.

When you truly change: You can experience the following things.

1. Your Circle Changes

People may say, "You've changed."

You haven't become arrogant—you've grown.

2. Financial Independence Develops

You rely less on others.

3. A New Tribe Appears

You attract higher-level thinkers.

4. Opportunities Expand

Alignment creates access.

5. **Speech Becomes Disciplined**

You stop speaking negatively.

6. **Reflection Replaces Impulse**

Wisdom grows.

7. **Learning Replaces Mimicry**

You study instead of copying.

8. **You Master the Power of "No"**

You protect your time and energy.

The Law of Reflection

As you learn to respect and love yourself, the world reflects it back.

Become Your Own Role Model – Action Plan

1. **Circle Evaluation**

List 5 closest people.

Ask:

- Do they inspire growth?
- Do they drain energy?

Gradually reduce negative influence.

2. **Financial Independence Plan**

    - Track expenses for 30 days.
    - Build 6-month emergency fund.
    - Invest in skill development.

3. **3The "No" Practice**

This week

Say "No" to:

- One distraction
- One unnecessary commitment
- One comfort habit

4. Speech Discipline

For 7 days:

- No gossip
- No complaining
- No negative self-talk

Your True Mission

Continuously strengthen your mind and body to sustain success.

Final 90-Day Transformation Blueprint

From Identity to Mastery

"Transformation is not an event.

It is a decision repeated every day."

How To Use This Blueprint

This is not a motivational plan.

This is a **system**.

Every day you will work on **3 levels of transformation**:

1. **Identity (Who you are becoming)**
2. **Action (What you do daily)**
3. **Discipline (What you avoid)**

PHASE 1 (DAY 1–30) — IDENTITY & CLARITY

Build Self-Realisation and Direction

Focus: Chapter 1, 2, 3

(Self-Realisation, Time, Direction)

Primary Objective

- Understand yourself
- Remove confusion
- Build clarity

Daily Non-Negotiable

- 20 min reading
- 10 min silence
- 20 min physical movement
- Write your goal daily

WEEK 1: SELF-REALISATION

Tasks

- Write **10 personal qualities**
- Identify **3 core skills**
- Answer:
  - Who am I beyond my job?
  - What is my real strength?

Night Question

"Did my actions match the person I want to become?"

WEEK 2: FUTURE IDENTITY

Tasks

- Write a **10-year vision letter**
- Define:
  - Income
  - Health
  - Discipline

    - Lifestyle

- Fix **one primary goal**

Example

"Become debt-free in 18 months."

WEEK 3: TIME CONTROL (8×8×8 RULE)

Structure Your Day

- 8 hrs sleep
- 8 hrs work
- 8 hrs growth

Golden 8 Focus

- Skill building
- Health
- Planning

Eliminate

- Unnecessary scrolling
- Time-wasting habits

WEEK 4: DIRECTION & FOCUS

7-Day Reset

- Delete unnecessary apps
- Limit entertainment to 1 hour
- Work in 45-min focus blocks
- Avoid negative people

Sunday Review

- What moved me forward?
- What distracted me?

PHASE 2 (DAY 31–60) — DISCIPLINE & CONTROL

Build Strength and Consistency

Focus: Chapter 4, 5, 6

(Intention, Discipline, Happiness)

PRIMARY OBJECTIVE

- Control impulses
- Build discipline
- Purify intention

DAILY NON-NEGOTIABLES

- Fixed wake-up time
- 45–60 min workout
- 1 hour focused work
- 10 min reflection

WEEK 5: PURE INTENTION

Ask Daily

- Why am I doing this?
- Is this honest growth?

Rules

- No shortcuts
- No manipulation

- Focus on value creation

WEEK 6: DISCIPLINE CHALLENGE (START 30 DAYS)

Choose ONLY 3 habits

- Fixed wake-up time
- Daily exercise
- 1-hour deep work

NB-No compromise

WEEK 7: DOPAMINE RESET

Avoid

- Social media excess
- Junk content
- Mindless scrolling

Replace

- Reading
- Walking

- Learning

WEEK 8: HAPPINESS CONTROL

Daily Practice

- 20 min exercise
- 20 min learning
- 10 min silence

Reflection

- Which habits give temporary pleasure?
- What are they costing my future?

PHASE 3 (DAY 61–90) — EXPANSION & IDENTITY SHIFT

Become Your New Self

Focus: Chapter 7, 8

(Mind Alignment, Role Model)

PRIMARY OBJECTIVE

- Align mind with goals
- Upgrade environment
- Become self-driven

DAILY NON-NEGOTIABLES

- Workout (intense)
- Goal visualization
- Learning (30 min)
- Night review

WEEK 9: MIND ALIGNMENT

Practices

- Create vision board
- Set goal wallpaper
- Write goal daily

Rule

Do not force the mind — align it.

WEEK 10: MICRO-WINS SYSTEM

Break Goals

- Monthly target
- Weekly target
- Daily action

Celebrate Progress

Small wins = strong mindset

WEEK 11: ENVIRONMENT UPGRADE

Circle Evaluation

Ask:

- Who inspires me?
- Who drains me?

NB-Reduce negative influence

WEEK 12: BECOME YOUR ROLE MODEL

Build These Traits

- Financial awareness
- Speech discipline
- Emotional control
- Decision clarity

Practice

- Say "NO" to distractions
- No gossip
- No complaining

FINAL 7 DAYS — TRANSFORMATION LOCK-IN

Hard Week Challenge

- Wake early daily
- Workout daily
- No distractions
- Strict routine

Deep Reflection

- Who was I 90 days ago?
- Who am I now?
- What has changed?

DAILY TRACKER (SIMPLE SYSTEM)

✓ Workout

✓ Learning

✓ Discipline maintained

✓ Goal-focused action

✓ No unnecessary distractions

THE FINAL REALISATION

After 90 days, you will not just have:

- Better habits
- Better health
- Better focus

You will have a **new identity**

FINAL MESSAGE.

"You don't become successful by chance.
You become successful by design."

"Your life changes the moment you decide
to become the person your goals require."